I0826760

he

a collection of original poetry

by Terry a. O'Neal

LeBleu Publishing

First edition

Published in 2026 by
LeBleu Publishing

ISBN 978-0-9679446-2-3

Library of Congress Control Number: 2017904097

Printed in the United States of America

978-0-9679446-2-3
Imprint: LeBleu Publishing

I would rather have his heart for eternity than

his soul for a lifetime.

Contents

Foreword

This book was born out of listening.

Listening to the quiet strength of Black men whose stories rarely make it into the pages of books, whose struggles often go unnamed, and whose tenderness is too often hidden beneath the weight of expectation. *He* is not a single man. *He* is many men. *He* is the son, the father, the lover, the protector, the dreamer, the wounded, the warrior, and the quiet soul who keeps going when the world has given him every reason to stop.

For generations, Black men in America have carried burdens both visible and unseen. History remembers them in fragments—sometimes as heroes, sometimes as suspects, sometimes as shadows—but rarely as whole men. Rarely as human beings whose lives are made of love, grief, longing, beauty, and contradiction. These poems attempt to stand beside that truth. They are not explanations. They are reflections.

In these pages, you will meet men who roar like thunder and men who whisper through pain. You will see the man who stands tall in the face of a world determined to break him, and the man who finds his strength only when he is able to lay his burdens down for a moment in the arms of someone who loves him. You will see the scars history leaves behind and the quiet ways a man rebuilds himself when no one is watching.

Some of these poems speak of struggle—of racism, violence, expectation, and the long shadow of slavery that still lingers across American life.

Others speak of love, devotion, fatherhood, and spiritual connection. Together they form a portrait not of perfection, but of humanity.

He is also about relationship. The way men love. The way they protect. The way they endure. The way they sometimes fall silent when the world refuses to hear them. Many of the poems in this collection were written while watching the men in my life—sons, brothers, fathers, friends—move through a world that demands strength from them at every turn. I have watched them rise. I have watched them struggle. And I have watched them keep walking forward.

That is where these poems live: in that space between vulnerability and resilience.

This book is a tribute, but it is also a witness. A reminder that behind every statistic, every headline, every stereotype, there is a life unfolding—complex, fragile, magnificent. A life that deserves to be seen in its fullness.

And so, these poems say what is too often left unsaid:

Black men are worthy of love.
They are worthy of grace.
They are worthy of being understood.

Most of all, they are worthy of being heard.

—Terry A. O'Neal

Dedicated to James Alphonse of Chloe.

he

I. Spirit

"Before I formed thee in the belly I knew thee."
—Jeremiah, Book of Jeremiah 1:5

Tomorrow is

tomorrow is made for those, who discover what yesterday
held close to her bosom beneath a blue cloth
wailing chants flutter on moth wings to the moon

waking and walking in pitch-blackness of day
balancing a tightrope wearing lofty hope
wailing chants flutter on moth wings to the moon

a mystery left unsolved to bygone days
and unpaved shallow roads bearing the raw truth
masked dance on dormant dreams weeps a lowly croon

a folktale adorned with obscure reflections
in murky waters at the edge of a bayou
wailing chants flutter on moth wings to the moon

blind to the twisting, turning, spiraling storm
ripping through the heartbeats of promise unseen
masked dance on dormant dreams weeps a lowly croon

a thief out to satisfy its thirsty soul
bearing no mercy for what is destined near
old spirits bask in quiet reverie while
wailing chants flutter on moth wings to the moon

Circle of Eternity

his excellence emerges
from many places
untold faces of wisdom
deep-rooted in the earth
fresh soil yielding crops of love
and jagged-edged tenderness
notwithstanding
the wintry mists
resting upon the shoulders
of thirty mountain tops

in high regard
I hold him

solid character:
vast depth, soaring height—
the stunning beauty of a man
of black serpentine

1960 markings carefully etched
tell a narrative:
a reflection of past suffering,
passion, and purpose

aesthetic expressions
draw me nearer

ancient bond between souls
fastened by the sun

between verses
h/e is
the main clause
completing my fragmented thoughts—

in all his splendor
standing alone
he makes a thunderous statement:

hear him roar

in my weakness
he is strong

beyond existence
I have loved him
like a circle

infinite is he –

together
we are one

He

is simple, yet complex.

His movements
are difficult to comprehend
at times.

An undying passion
burns deep within his soul
beneath layers
of heartbreak.

Like shattered glass
we glimpse only fragments
of his life.

Tiny shards left behind
mark the pain, the struggle,
the emptiness—
igniting his desire
for something greater.

Armored,
protector of his own spirit,
for to shed that armor
would leave him exposed
to the cold world.

His heart bleeds
through half-mooned smiles
that often go unnoticed

because no one truly sees
his struggle—

no one
really knows
his story

Channels to the Black Sea

A cowardly speck,
too minute to be seen
beneath a microscopic lens:

he who chooses
narrow triumph
over integrity and honor
travels a hazardous road
to nothingness.

Not even the seeds
in his garden
will bloom
in the fresh soil
of his footsteps—

for darkness
cannot yield
wholesomeness.

Little need be spoken
of the heedful listener:

the lofty, courageous man
who steps
with unceasing purpose,
ushered forward
to his destiny.

So Much Depends

so much depends
upon

a Black man

standing
his ground

holding together
what others

have broken

for it is
the hardest work

even a long line
of self-serving men

could never
undertake

let alone

with such
bold
eloquence

Dance. A Song.

We have known each other
all our lives,
connected by the rhythm
of one pulse.

At the core
our spirits fuse.

Songs of the warrior
and melodies of the goddess
move through us,

dancing
around the burning flames,
gliding upward
to the silvery moon.

Walk That Walk

Talk that talk, brother!
Preach it—say it!

There's conviction
in yo' stride.

You sayin', speakin',
prayin' and preachin'—

Then walk that walk, brother!

Walk it tall.
Walk it wide.

II. Struggle

"I am a man."
—Martin Luther King, Jr.

The Negro Son

I was born a slave.

Put on the block,
bought and sold
several times
in a single day—

snatched away
from my mother,
separated
from my sister
and brother.

Almighty God,
will I ever
see my family again?

Bagged, tagged, tied up,
roped to the rear
of a horse,
walking for miles
in the blazing sun.

Almighty God,
am I not Your son?

Wondering
what will become of me,
will I ever see
beyond this misery—

less worth
than the stray dog
that trails behind me?

From the dirt
which I have come –

am I not a man,
Almighty God?

Am I not
Your son?

Nights in Birmingham

Every night
like the Fourth of July

firebomb sparks
light up the sky.

Dark smoke clouds
fill the air
as all the small children
stop and stare.

The daddies yell in anger,
the mommies scream in fear,
with wretched cries so shrill
they pierce the ear.

And all the while
the White man's laugh
lingers

near
          near
                    nearer
...

until

his laugh

lingers

here.

Clank, Clank Go My Shoes

I. The Journey

Take everything I own.
Your property is my flesh—
skin
and bone.

Locked up,
a poor tangled soul,
my battered spirit
stolen,
lost
in obscurity.

Clank, clank
clank, clank
go my shoes.

For you know not
the secrets
that lie within me.

Behind closed doors
in reverie
I see the North Star—

so close…
so far.

Clank, clank
clank, clank
go my shoes.

Freedom lies within,
far beneath the surface
of my own skin.

I follow
behind my dream.

Though I stumble
and fall,
pant
and brawl
through icy waters,
up the high mountain
I crawl.

Clank, clank
clank, clank
go my shoes.

Toward the bright light
I reach my hand.

On the steps
of the safe house
I stand.

Miles and miles
of blackness
cover the barren land.

I tread softly—

barefoot.
...
...

go my shoes.

II. The Burial

Under the ground,
six feet below,
covered in dirt
from head
to toe—

I've been buried alive.

For every time I tried,
for every lie
I let pass by,
for every tear,
for every sigh—

I've been buried alive.

From rejection,
every slap in the face,
from every race,
from the guns
and drugs,
from temptation,
from love—

I've been buried alive.

From every right way I turn,
from every left
I get burned.

From every dime I make,
for all the shit
that I take,
for all the hate—

I've been buried alive.

III. The World Above

From every bomb flying,
every child crying,
every son
that lay dying—

I've been buried alive.

From every saint
condemning me,
sentenced to life
without parole,

locked behind
the bars
of my soul—

I've been buried alive.

From yesterday
and today,
from tomorrow's dismay,
from not wanting
to see
another day—

I have been buried alive.

I've been buried alive.

I

have

been

buried

alive

I Am

Barely enough strength left to stand
hoping against hope
in a battle for your life—
dreams beaten down, staggering,
falling against the rope.

Am I my sister's keeper,
my brother's fortress,
his refuge from the storm?

Whatever happened to that village
that steered the young,
reared our children,
and lifted hope for tomorrow
and brighter days to come?

Sound—
breaking barriers of light,
the echoes of the old
can penetrate stone,
yet cannot change
perception or sight.

Colorism, birthed from slavery.
The lack of knowledge
continues to suppress me—
bamboozled into believing
what outsiders claim is my truth,
who I'm supposed to be.
For half of what you see
is illusion.

Until you live a day in this life
you cannot identify with
my agony
or my strife.

Lead by example, they say
based on what we see each day.
Mama is caught
between stone
and harder place,
while Daddy runs
a losing race,
left to wonder
where his fate will lie.

Am I my sister's keeper,
my brother's fortress,
his refuge from the storm?

Time moves steady,
ticking away too fast.
Idle and crestfallen minds
set the stage for rage
and self-destructive ways.

Lost, searching for a cause,
mis-under-stood.
Outward visions
poison the mind,
concealed behind
a hood of transgression,
sinking deeper and deeper

into oppression
held captive
by one's own mind.

Products of our everyday,
put in restraints
to keep us from flourishing,
taught to believe
we can only achieve
so much—
or so little.

Street signs read:
"Stop. Don't Shoot".
"Go."
"Slow Ahead."
"Yield."
"Caution."
"No Hunting Allowed Without Permission"

Yet every day
is open season
in the hood—
no license required.

It seems my life
Is not worth saving,
depreciating by the second,
reduced, devalued,
and at times
annihilated
by my very own.

Am I my sister's keeper,
my brother's fortress,
his refuge from the storm?

the more things change,
the more they stay same.
And in the end
the White man wins—
because this is what he intended
us to be:
dead upon arrival.

Unless we change shape,
redirect the path,
expand knowledge,
heal—rebuild
a culture of unity
and become more.

Not "Am I?',
but I Am.

I am my sister's keeper,
my brother's fortress,
his refuge from the storm.

I am.

Restless Royalty

An abounding heart of pain
traveled with him
from place to place,
like a tilted crown
forever seeking
its castle.

The Impatient Reader

She wasn't the prettiest story.

Fear and bitterness
pushed her through the climax.

Peeking ahead,
she knew what waited
on the other side.

Though the road before her
would be thorny,
the promise
was worth the pain.

And so
the pages turned

as she journeyed
through the falling action
toward the horizon.

Poet's Dream

It's a thorny road

for dreamers and poets

who fantasize of majestic places and

deep-seated desires of the heart

that their hands may never hold.

III. Love

"Infinite love is the truest narrative."
—Terry A. O'Neal

Restoration

The only time
he laughed out loud
was in her arms.
There he laid down
his burdens upon her,
gathering strength
to go out
and weather the storm
again.

Listen Man

There are some things
a woman—a
strong-minded Black wombman—
simply can't come back from.

Some things
an "I'm sorry, baby"
cannot mend.

Cryin' shoulda, coulda, wouldas,
Reflecting on tranquil walks at dusk
And tiny moon glints in my eyes.

My feelings, tangled and knotted
like my kinky-curly hair at the roots,
saturated by storm,
unearthing the natural truth—
neither which is impartial.

If Not with You

If he
cannot share
his vulnerabilities
with whom
he so loves,
he cannot
reveal them
to anyone.

Abstract I Love Yous

In his absence,
I am unhinged.

The absence of his spirit,
the absence of his firm touch—
the absence of his heart,
his harsh kiss,
his fragmented voice
drilling in my ear,

abstract *I love yous,*
though he refuses
to say it
twice.

Scratching at Sunrise

ripped in two unequal parts,
she scours the earth
searching for a dead-end road
where intimate thoughts
can be abandoned.

afraid to close her eyes
where his voice echoes—
forbidden territory
invaded by dreams
set adrift.

"nothing's fair in the world.
nothing is safe—"
a harsh reality
battering her
again and again.

desperately seeking diversions
to pass motionless time,
for he who dwells within
she must somehow
disregard.

She shakes loose
tiny fragments of him
from her spirit,
bit by bit,
falling into a pit
of make-believe
and imitation.

the imagination is boundless.
fears and endless tears

reveal her grief
as she lies alone in darkness
in the stillness of night.

scratching away at sunrise
to birth a brand-new day—
one that might be
ever-so kind
and merciful
enough to carry
her troubles away.

A Love Story of Sorts

All those who lost shall weep,
for rare jewels
don't come cheap.

Like her,
it was his second chance at life,
a second chance at love.

He prayed for her,
and so it was.

She made herself vulnerable to him,
vast—
like wide-open space
engulfed by the wind.

All those who passed her by
could not see beyond
her dreary night skies.

But in the land he loved
he found her spirit
in all its glory.

She was his jewel
in the rough,
one he would polish
and keep
as his own.

All those who lost shall weep,
for rare jewels
don't come cheap.

And he knew
he was a rich man—

for there was no jewel
quite like her
in all the ancient land.

Weightless

Head in the clouds,
you are the sun that breaks through.
Thoughts of you
stir in my mind
time after time—
when I rise,
when I fall,
through it all.

You are the smile
upon my lips,
the sway of my hips,
the thump beating
in my chest,
leaving me
weightless.

You are the glisten
in my eye,
the air in my stride—
light on my feet.

You are the hope
that floats within me,
the constant
that tells me
this is real
and not just
a fantasy.

I inhale
your body's fragrance,
every inch

from head to toe—
slow.

Because I know
this love
is everlasting.

Because the world
stops spinning
when I am with you.

And if it's the last thing
I ever do,
I will hold on,
be still,
and wait.

Tragedy

I loved him
to the bottom
of my soul.

He was everything
I ever wanted,
but never had
the pleasure
to hold.

She

You are the beauty
that is through, to my heart--
everything I do,
I do for you.
My beautiful, Black Queen,
my love for you is infinite
as I yearn to one day
be your provider again.

My heart, too, aches
from the abuse I am forced
to watch upon you.

I pretend
not to love you more
because of my shame.
But just this once
I must be true:
It is you I love,
and pray that love
will set you free.
I desire this
more than life itself.
If you know nothing else,
know this, my Queen,
we will rise again.

-- A poem for her, he wrote.
(circa 2015)

The best narrative is one of infinite love: a spiritual affair—not of the material world, with no beginning and no end. It will always stand the test of time.

IV. Reflection

"When love takes root in the human heart, no force on earth can uproot it."

—James Baldwin

In the End

Maybe she will be broken forever,
but if it is so
she will adorn it
with radiant elegance.

And all that man
will ever discern
is her effortless grace
and the softness
of her smile.

Reflections in C Major

It lies deep within her marrow—
tiny fragments
that remain constant.

He is an extension of her.

Without him
the air is dry and still,
and there is no light.

In his eyes
is her reflection.

As the universe
plays its prelude in C major,
her love for him
remains endless.

For even when time
moves on,
one quiet truth remains:
he was always
a part of her.

Infinite Love

In spring,
I cradled him in my arms.
Behold—a son, my firstborn king,
the first love of my life,
keeper of my heart,
pressed to solve every problem,
my glimmer of light,
my always forever.

In winter,
his spirit was a gift—
strong-willed one,
my second-born son,
King Two.

He carries me
when I am weak,
the second love of my life,
keeping hope alive
in times of strife.

And again,
on the three hundred sixty-fifth day,
in a reflection of light
emerged a blessing in disguise—
an uncut love
before my eyes.

A princess, inconceivable.
Our hearts beat as one.

More than life
and living in it,

I treasure her—
I treasure them
always.

One More River of Rain

One more river of rain before I go,
Crossing over Cessford
and North Booker row.

Tuesday night's storm
wash away the strongholds
and the chains
that keep me bound.

The sins of the father
trickle down to the son.
What will become
of my salvation
if hope is never won?

What can an ol' believer do
to crush the giant
Stomping his back in two?

Just return me
to the joy
when I was a little boy.

Before the sun shall rise
pour one more river of rain
before I die.

Let it fall on broken ground,
let it cleanse this weary soul,
let it carry sorrow
where troubled waters roll.

And if mercy finds me
Somewhere in that flood,

wash the dust from my feet
and the sorrow from my blood.

Before the morning light,
before the last goodbye—
Lord, send one more river of rain
before I die.

Doormat

Birds sing to the wind chimes
hanging from the limbs of a tree,
while the neighbor's dog cries wolf
through gaps between the pickets.
It's that time again.
Sweetness fills the air.

I stare from an open window
through tiny holes in the screen
as she rough handles it
like a disobedient child—
shaking it hard,
battering it with the handle
of her feeble broomstick
to chase away the pesky dust mites
that gathered last fall.

after hours playing tug-of-war
they've had enough,
a truce is called.
both lose
again.

so she hung it on the line to rest,
absorbing the freshness of outdoors
and the energy of the sun.

well-worn with smudges
and soiled boot prints,
the stench of fried fish
and the soot of drunken tales
slowly drift away,
floating in the wind with pollen

from shrub to shrub
to the next—

only to return again
a brand-new crop
of boot prints
next spring.

On the Battlefield in Mobile
For Ms. Beulah Mae Donald

Not so long ago,
1962,
a brown baby boy
was born
in Mobile.

His name
was Michael.

Along a dark
southern road
wanders the soul
of a young Black man,

Yes,
he is a brother of mine.

His name
was Michael Donald.

Not so long ago,
1981,
somewhere in Alabama
a lynching took place,
devastating the entire Black race.

His name
was Michael.

Footprints remain
of a brave colored soldier

with a dream yet to be,
crying,

"What does America mean to me?"

Rise and sing, my people!

Yes,
he is a brother of mine.

His name
was Michael Donald.

Many folks prayed,
many folks sighed
the day that brother Michael
lay down on the battlefield
and died.

O brothers, O sisters—
not so long ago,
March 1981,
One Saturday evening
another soul
was set free.

Along the dark,
southern road
there stands the spirit
of a young Black man.

Yes,
he is a brother of mine.

His name
is Michael Donald.

Written November 2005

In the busyness of living, he is the kind of man that makes a woman pause and write romantic poetry.

About the Author

Terry a. O'Neal was born in French Camp, California, and raised in Stockton, where she grew up in a household shaped by creativity, resilience, and the quiet power of storytelling. Her mother, Barbara Ann Tillman-Williams, a Louisiana native, filled the home with poetry, culture, literature, and art, nurturing a love of language that would eventually guide O'Neal toward her life as a writer.

Though she was raised in California, O'Neal's roots run deep in the South. Her maternal lineage traces back to Calcasieu Parish, Louisiana, where generations of her family lived on historic LeBleu Settlement in Chloe. Her grandparents, great-grandparents, and ancestors before them were born on that land, working the soil, raising families, and building lives in a place that carries both struggle and memory. The stories of that place—passed down through family and history—have quietly shaped much of her writing.

Poetry has always been O'Neal's first language. Influenced by the voices of the Harlem Renaissance, including Langston Hughes, Gwendolyn Brooks, and Carolyn M. Rodgers, her work reflects both the cultural depth of the Black experience and the universal search for meaning, dignity, and love. As a young girl, she had the opportunity to meet Maya Angelou at the art gallery where her mother worked, a moment that left a lasting impression and strengthened her belief in the power of words to shape lives.

Over the years, O'Neal has written across multiple genres, including poetry, fiction, children's literature, and screenwriting. Her books include several collections of poetry as well as the coming-of-age novel Sweet Lavender, a story rooted in themes of family, resilience, and the search for belonging. Her poetry has appeared in journals and publications throughout the United States and internationally.

Alongside her writing, O'Neal has devoted much of her life to mentoring young voices. Through her youth anthology series *Make Some Noise!,* she has helped publish the work of young writers from across the country, encouraging adolescents to find strength in their stories and confidence in their words. She has also founded and led several nonprofit initiatives dedicated to youth education and cultural awareness, including the National Black History Bee, a program designed to engage students in the study of African American history.

Today, O'Neal's work continues to evolve as she explores the connections between literature, history, and ancestral memory. In 2026 she founded the Chloe African American Cemetery Preservation Association, an organization dedicated to protecting and honoring a historic burial ground in Chloe, Louisiana, where generations of African American families—including her own ancestors—were laid to rest. The work of restoring and preserving that sacred ground is deeply personal to her and reflects her belief that storytelling is not only written on the page but also preserved in the land and in the lives of those who came before us.

As a poet, O'Neal writes from a place where history, love, struggle, and memory meet. Her work often explores the complexity of Black identity, the strength of family, and the enduring humanity that binds us together.

She believes the most powerful stories are those rooted in truth, memory, and love—and that the voices of those who came before us still echo in the stories we tell today.

Terry a. O'Neal, Garches, Île-de-France
April 6, 2025 | Photograph by Thai Ng

Because of Her, My Mother

My mother was the first voice that shaped my understanding of the world. Long before I ever wrote a poem, she was teaching me the language of compassion and love through the way she spoke, the way she listened, the way she carried herself with quiet strength. From her I learned that tenderness is not weakness, and that love, when lived honestly, is its own kind of courage.

She poured into my heart the very words that would one day find their way onto these pages.

My mother left this earth on February 22, 2019. I long for her still in the physical sense, in those ordinary ways a daughter longs for her mother's presence.

Yet, there are moments when I feel her just as clearly as ever, moving gently through the spiritual spaces of my life, reminding me of who I am, the lessons she taught me, and where I come from.

If there is anything worthy in these poems—any compassion, any reverence for life, any measure of grace—it was first planted by her hands.

All the great I am is because of her.

www.ingramcontent.com/pod-product-compliance
Lightning Source LLC
LaVergne TN
LVHW050609100826
845148LV00015B/3197

9780967944623